WHEN LIFE GIVES YOU LEMONS... ...MAKE ORANGE JUICE

When life gives you lemons... ...make orange juice

A different view of life

ISABELLA THORNE

Sunduq

~ 1 ~

INTRODUCTION

Life is a blank canvas waiting to be painted. At first, the canvas can be intimidating, and you might not know where to begin. But with each stroke of the brush, the picture becomes clearer, and your vision comes to life.

Like a canvas, life requires patience and persistence. It takes time to create a work of art, and sometimes you need to step back and look at the bigger picture. You might make mistakes, but you can always paint over them and start again.

As you paint your canvas, you'll face challenges and obstacles. Sometimes the colors won't mix the way you want them to, or the brush won't do what you want it to. But these challenges teach you to be adaptable, and you'll learn new techniques along the way.

Every brush stroke adds depth and character to your canvas. Some strokes are bold and vibrant, while others are soft and subtle. Each stroke is unique and adds to the overall beauty of the painting.

But remember, you don't have take life too seriously all the time. Be bold. Be different; and when life gives you lemons, you go ahead and make orange juice!

~ 2 ~

CHAPTER 1

Be your own boss

Self-control is like trying not to eat a whole tray of brownies at once. One time, my friend Sarah and I went to a party where there were dozens of brownies on display. Sarah went wild and took a whole bunch, but I tried to control myself and only took one. It wasn't easy, but I didn't want to end up feeling sick and regretful like I did last time I binged on brownies.

Self-control can also mean resisting the temptation to cheat or copy someone else's work, which I've definitely been tempted to do before. But I knew that it wouldn't be fair to others, and I didn't want to get in trouble with the teacher.

Be your own boss...
To improve your self-control, you can practice mindfulness, which I've found really helpful in avoiding distractions and staying focused. It's also important to set realistic goals, like limiting your screen time or sticking to a study schedule. And when you're tempted to give in to temptation, remind yourself that self-control is like a muscle that gets stronger with practice.

For instance, let's say you're at a party and everyone is smoking weed. You might feel like you should join in to fit in but remember that drugs can have serious consequences. So instead of giving in to peer pressure, try to find a way to excuse yourself from the situation. It's not easy, but it's the responsible choice.

Decide what's important for you...

Self-control is an important skill that can help you make smart choices and avoid trouble. By practicing mindfulness, setting goals, and resisting temptation, you can become a better, more responsible person.

Setting priorities is like choosing between eating a healthy salad or a greasy pizza. When I was in school, I loved playing video games, but I also knew that I had to finish my homework first. It wasn't always easy, but setting priorities helped me manage my time better and avoid getting in trouble with my parents and teachers.

Don't fall into the trap...

Avoiding temptation is like resisting the urge to watch an entire season of your favorite show in one night. One time, my friends wanted to sneak into an R-rated movie, but I knew it wasn't a good idea. I exercised self-control and convinced them to watch a different movie instead. It wasn't easy, but it saved us from getting kicked out and grounded.

Be easy on yourself...

Forgiving yourself is like forgiving yourself for eating too many cookies. We all make mistakes, and I once forgot to do an important assignment for school. Instead of beating myself up over it, I forgave myself and worked hard to earn a good grade on the assignment.

In life, it's important to set priorities, avoid temptation, and forgive yourself for mistakes. By managing your time, resisting peer pressure, and learning from your mistakes, you can become a better and happier person. And who knows, you might even find a few laughs along the way!

~ 3 ~

CHAPTER 2

What doesn't kill me, only makes me stronger

Failure is a part of life, and it's something we all encounter at one time or another. When I was growing up, I used to dread failing. I thought it was the worst thing that could happen to me. I didn't want to be seen as a failure or disappoint anyone. But over time, I realized that failure is not something to be ashamed of; it's an opportunity to learn.

One of the best lessons I learned from failure is that it can teach you more than success ever could. When things are going well, it's easy to get complacent and not push yourself. But when you fail, you have to take a step back, reassess, and try again. Failure forces you to look at things from a different perspective and come up with new solutions.

For instance, one time, I was preparing for a school talent show, and I decided to sing a song I'd written. I practiced and practiced until I thought I had it down. But when the day of the show arrived, I got up on stage, and my mind went blank. I couldn't remember the words to my song. I was mortified, but I learned a valuable lesson that day. I learned that failure can happen to anyone, no matter how prepared or confident they may feel.

It's important to remember that failure is not something to be feared. Instead, it should be embraced as a natural part of the learning process. When you fail, take a step back, reflect on what went wrong, and come up with a new plan. And don't be afraid to ask for help or guidance along the way.

So, the next time you encounter failure, remember that you're in good company. Everyone fails at some point in their lives. But it's how you respond to failure that defines you. Use it as an opportunity to learn, grow, and ultimately succeed.

Failure, huh? Even the word sounds ominous, like some kind of dark cloud hanging over your head. But as someone who has faced her fair share of failures, let me tell you that it's not as scary as it seems. Failure isn't the end of the world, it's just a little blip in the grand scheme of things.

Sure, failure can be uncomfortable, and it's easy to worry about what others will think. But here's the thing: the more you fail, the more you learn. And those lessons will serve you well the next time you face a challenge. It's all about embracing failure as an opportunity to do better next time.

Of course, it's easier said than done. Negative self-talk can be a real buzzkill. You know the kind of thing I'm talking about: "I'm no good, not smart enough, unworthy." But let's be real here - would you talk to a friend that way? Of course not! So why do it to yourself? Instead, talk to yourself like you would to a friend. "That was a great idea! You'll do better next time."

Accepting failure isn't always easy. It's uncomfortable and sometimes downright painful. But it's also necessary if you want to grow and become a better, stronger person. Here are some steps to help you make peace with failure:

Acknowledge your failures. Don't sweep them under the rug or pretend they didn't happen.

Take responsibility for your actions. Own up to your mistakes and learn from them.

Reflect on what went wrong. What could you have done differently? What did you learn?

Use what you've learned to do better next time. Remember, failure is just an opportunity to do something again, only better.

Failure like an unexpected pop quiz or a pimple on picture day - not fun, but not the end of the world. I used to be scared of failing, but then I realized that failure is just a part of the journey. And trust me, I've had my fair share of failures.

The first step in dealing with failure is acknowledging it. It's like finally admitting that you ate the entire bag of chips by yourself - not pretty, but necessary. It's hard to learn from your mistakes if you don't admit them. Plus, it feels pretty good to get it off your chest. You can even make it a group therapy session and invite your friends over for some pizza and a good old-fashioned pity party.

Once you've acknowledged your failure, it's time to examine your feelings. It's like cleaning up after a party - it's not fun, but it has to be done. You might feel disappointed, angry, confused, or sad. But don't worry, it's all part of the process. Embrace those feelings, and then let them go. You can even write a break-up letter to your failure - "Dear Failure, it's not me, it's you. You just weren't right for me."

Now it's time to talk to someone about it. It's like getting a second opinion from a friend before sending that risky text. Talk to a friend, a family member, or a trusted adult. They might have some great advice or a different perspective. Plus, it's always nice to have someone to commiserate with over a pint of ice cream or a bag of sour gummy worms. When we first learned to ride a bike, we probably fell off a few times before we got the hang of it. But we didn't let those failures stop us from eventually riding with confidence and ease. Just like riding a bike, failure is a natural part of the learning process. It's not something to be afraid of, but rather something to embrace and learn from.

In the world of music, failure can sometimes lead to unexpected success. Take the story of Elvis Presley, for example. Early in his career, he was told by a music producer that he should give up and go back to driving a truck. But Elvis didn't let that failure define him. He kept working at his craft, experimenting with new styles and sounds, and eventually became one of the most iconic musicians of all time.

Lessons to learn from failure include failing forward. Every mistake is an opportunity to learn and improve. It's not about the number of times you fall down, but rather the number of times you get back up and keep going. Failure is not an end, but rather a new beginning.

It tests our resilience and shows exactly what we are made of. It's important to find healthy ways to cope with disappointment and to learn from our mistakes. By doing so, we can build confidence and self-esteem, and develop the ability to tackle any challenge that comes our way.

It's important to express our honest feelings about our failures, whether that's with friends, family, or a trusted mentor. By doing so, we can gain valuable feedback and support, and ultimately become more emotionally mature.

Remember, failure is not something to be afraid of, but rather a natural part of the journey to success. Embrace your failures, learn from them, and keep moving forward.

~ 4 ~

CHAPTER 3

The choice is yours

Never let anyone tell you that your life is not in your hands. You always have a choice and it's up to you how you shape your life. Knowing that the choices that you make in life can affect everyone around you, that's why it is so important to know how to make the right decisions. This is where I come in...

As a young woman, I've learned that decision-making is a vital part of growing up. It's about making choices that are not only wise, but also aligned with your values and principles.

As with most of us, my parents made most of my decisions for me when I was younger. They guided me on what to wear, what to eat, and who to spend time with. However, as I got older, I began to make more decisions for myself. It was challenging at first, but it taught me a lot about responsibility and independence.

Some decisions were black and white. It is clear that stealing, cheating, and hurting others were wrong, while being honest, kind, and respectful were the right things to do. However, as I grew older, I realized that some decisions were not so straightforward. There were situations where I had to choose between multiple options, and it wasn't always clear which one was the best. This is where good decision-making skills come into play.

As a writer, I often find myself in situations where I'm not sure what the right decision is. For example, when writing a book, I might struggle to decide which character should live or die or what direction the plot should take. In situations like this, I've learned that good decision-making skills are crucial.

One of the most helpful ways to approach a complicated decision is to seek advice from someone you trust. This could be a friend, a family member, or a mentor. They can provide a different perspective that you might not have considered and help you make a more informed decision.

Another approach is to weigh the pros and cons of each option. List out the potential benefits and drawbacks of each decision, and then evaluate them. This process can help you see the long-term consequences of your choices and make a more informed decision.

Why bother...?

Sometimes, it's tempting to avoid making decisions altogether. It's easy to let someone else take charge and make choices for us, especially if the decision doesn't seem significant. For instance, if your dad asks, "What do you want for dinner?" and you have no preference, it's okay to say, "Anything is fine. You decide." In situations like these, deferring the decision to someone else is often perfectly acceptable.

However, when it comes to more critical decisions, it's essential to have an active say in the matter. Every decision you make, no matter how small or big, shapes your future and sets the tone for future decisions. It's crucial to have the confidence to make decisions that align with your values and principles.

Seeking advice from trusted people like your parents, siblings, or coaches can be helpful when making significant decisions. They can offer different perspectives that you may not have considered and guide you in the right direction. Ultimately, it's up to you to make the final decision. After weighing the pros and cons, taking the time to think it over, and considering the advice of others, you can make the decision on your own. Remember that decision-making is a skill that you can develop and improve over time, so don't be afraid to take charge and make choices that will shape your future.

Everyday decisions...

I've come to realize that decision-making is a skill that we develop throughout our lives. Sometimes it's easy, like choosing between vanilla or chocolate ice cream. But other times, it's more challenging, like deciding on a college major or a career path. The truth is, decision-making is a fundamental aspect of life, and it's important to learn how to make wise choices that align with our values and goals. However, when it comes to more important decisions, you need to take the time to consider your options. No, seriously, take your sweet time. Don't rush into a decision before you're ready. If you're used to making quick decisions without thinking, take a deep breath and give yourself some space to think things through.

Consider every possible outcome, weigh the pros and cons, and don't forget to ask for advice from trusted sources. And don't forget to inject some humor into the process! For example, maybe you're trying to decide which college to attend, and you make a pro/con list that ends up being fifty-fifty. You could always flip a coin, or you could decide based on which school has better campus food. (Hey, it's important!)

Decision-making doesn't have to be a bore. Embrace the small, quick decisions and take your time when it comes to the big ones. Remember to seek advice, weigh your options, and most importantly, inject some humor into the process. After all, life is too short to take everything seriously!

Plain Jane & Touchy Tom...

Okay, let me tell you a story about my friend, Jane. She's normally a pretty thoughtful person, but when it comes to decision-making, she can be a bit impulsive. One day, she decided to dye her hair bright pink without really thinking it through. Let's just say it wasn't her best look.

After that incident, Jane realized that she needed to work on her decision-making skills. She learned that being thoughtful means considering all sides of an issue, even if it's just deciding what color to dye your hair. So, she came up with a process to help her make better decisions.

First, she identified the issue she needed to decide on. Was it a good idea to dye her hair bright pink? Probably not. Next, she gathered relevant information by talking to friends and researching different hair dye options. She even consulted with a hair stylist to get a professional opinion.

Then, she made a list of possible solutions. Should she go for a more subtle shade of pink or stick with her natural color? After considering all the options, she finally made a decision that was best for her.

But Jane didn't stop there. She also learned the importance of self-control when it comes to decision-making. She realized that it's easy to act impulsively and make poor decisions when you're not thinking clearly. So, she practiced self-control in everyday situations, like not interrupting others when they're speaking and using polite manners.

Jane showed us that being a thoughtful decision-maker takes practice. It's important to gather information, consider all sides of an issue, and practice self-control. So, next time you're faced with a decision, take a page out of Jane's book and make sure you're considering all your options before you go and dye your hair bright pink.

Another important aspect of thoughtful decision-making is having tolerance and patience. Let me tell you about my friend Tom. He had a tendency to make decisions based on his emotions rather than logic. One day, he got into an argument with his best friend and decided to end their friendship without really thinking it through.

Later on, Tom realized that his lack of tolerance and patience had caused him to make a hasty decision. He learned that it's essential to consider all factors and sides of an issue before making a decision, especially when it involves relationships with others.

So, Tom started practicing tolerance and patience in everyday situations. For example, he practiced being more patient with his siblings when they annoyed him and tried to understand their perspective. He also learned to tolerate different viewpoints and opinions, even if they were different from his own.

Through this process, Tom became a more thoughtful decision-maker. He learned to take his time, seek advice, and consider all options before making a decision. And as a result, he made wiser choices that were more aligned with his values and goals.

Being a thoughtful decision-maker means considering all sides of an issue, practicing self-control, and having tolerance and patience. So, next time you're faced with a decision, take a deep breath, consider all your options, and remember that hasty decisions can lead to unwanted consequences.

~ 5 ~

CHAPTER 4

Your key to success

As a woman who's had her fair share of ups and downs, let me tell you that maintaining a positive attitude is crucial. But, fear not, my friends! There are ways to stay positive, even when life gets tough.

First and foremost, find your passion and pursue it. Life is too short to do things that don't bring us joy. Maybe you've always wanted to take a painting class or learn how to play the guitar. Whatever it is, go for it! You never know where it might lead you.

Here's how to infuse your life with happiness.

Doing things that bring you joy can do wonders for your overall well-being and mindset. Personally, I find solace in dancing around my living room to my favorite tunes. There's something magical about moving my body to the rhythm that lifts my spirits. Whether it's dancing, hiking, painting, or reading a good book, seek out activities that spark joy in your life and make time for them. By doing so, you'll give yourself a mental break from the stresses of life and reenergize your soul.

It's human nature to compare ourselves to others, but let me tell you, it's a trap. Comparing ourselves to others can lead to negative self-talk and self-doubt. Instead, focus on your own journey and celebrate your victories, no matter how small they may be.

Have you ever been in a situation where you felt totally misunderstood? Maybe you were upset about something, and your friend didn't seem to get why you were so worked up. Well, that's where empathy comes in. Empathy means putting yourself in someone else's shoes and trying to understand where they're coming from. It's like being a mind reader, but without the superpowers!

Now, onto setting goals. Here's a tip: don't try to be Superman or Wonder Woman. We all have limitations, and that's okay. Instead of trying to take on the world all at once, start small and work your way up. Maybe you want to be a famous musician or a top athlete. That's awesome! But instead of aiming to win a Grammy or an Olympic medal right off the bat, start by practicing your craft every day and setting achievable goals for yourself. Like my grandma always said, "Rome wasn't built in a day!"

Lastly, focus on the good things in your life. It's easy to get caught up in the negatives, but if you take a step back and look at the big picture, you'll find that there are plenty of positives to be grateful for.

Maintaining a positive attitude is all about finding your passion, engaging in activities you love, avoiding comparisons, and focusing on the good things in your life. Remember, life is too short to be anything but happy!

Set yourself some goals...

I remember when I was in high school, I had a goal to make the varsity soccer team. I worked hard for months, but when tryouts came around, I didn't make the team. I was devastated and thought about giving up on my dream. But then, I realized that I wasn't setting specific and realistic goals. I hadn't broken down the steps I needed to take to improve my skills and prepare for the tryouts. That experience taught me the importance of setting specific and achievable goals.

Step 1: Set Specific and Realistic Goals

The first step is to set specific and realistic goals. Write down what you want to achieve and be clear about the outcome you desire. For example, if you want to improve your grades, set a specific target like getting a B or an A in a specific subject. Also, make sure your goals are achievable and realistic. Don't set yourself up for disappointment by aiming for something that's beyond your capabilities.

Step 2: Plan and Prioritize

Once you have set your goals, it's important to make a plan and prioritize your tasks. Break down your goals into smaller, actionable steps and set deadlines for each of them. Use a planner or calendar to keep track of your progress and schedule your time wisely. Also, be sure to prioritize your tasks according to their level of importance and urgency.

Step 3: Stay Motivated and Celebrate

The final step is to stay motivated and celebrate your successes. Visualize yourself achieving your goals and stay focused on the end result. Stay positive and surround yourself with people who support and encourage you. And when you achieve your goals, celebrate your success! Treat yourself to something you enjoy or simply take a moment to reflect on your hard work and accomplishment.

Remember, with determination and hard work, you can accomplish anything you set your mind to!

~ 6 ~

CHAPTER 5

Say it how it is...

Communication is a crucial skill that can help you in all aspects of life, whether you're talking to friends, family, or colleagues. Effective communication is essential for building strong relationships and achieving your goals. Here are the top five tips for effective communication, with some humorous anecdotes to keep it interesting:

Tip 1: Listen actively

I once had a friend who was a terrible listener. Whenever I spoke, he'd interrupt me to talk about himself or completely tune me out. Needless to say, our conversations were pretty one-sided. Active listening means paying attention to what the other person is saying and showing that you understand their perspective. Trust me, it can make all the difference in a conversation.

Tip 2: Be Clear and Concise

Have you ever had a conversation with someone who just won't get to the point? It can be frustrating, right? When communicating, it's important to be clear and concise. Use simple language and avoid rambling on about irrelevant topics. Get to the point and be direct, but also be mindful of the other person's feelings.

Tip 3: Show Respect

Respect is a fundamental aspect of effective communication. One time, I accidentally interrupted my boss during a meeting, and he was not happy. Oops! Show respect to the other person by using polite language, avoiding interrupting, and being open-minded to different opinions. Remember that everyone has their own perspective and experiences, and showing respect can help build a positive relationship.

Tip 4: Use Body Language

Have you ever had a conversation with someone who was looking everywhere but at you? It's not the most comfortable feeling, right? Nonverbal communication, such as body language, can play a significant role in effective communication. Use appropriate eye contact, facial expressions, and gestures to convey your message and show interest in the conversation. Pay attention to the other person's body language, as well, to understand their feelings and reactions.

Tip 5: Practice Empathy

Empathy is the ability to understand and share the feelings of another person. Practicing empathy can help you build better relationships and communicate more effectively. I once had a roommate who was going through a tough time, and I tried to show empathy by listening to her and offering support. It helped us build a stronger bond and improved our communication overall.

Receiving Criticism...

Receiving criticism can be tough, but it's also an essential part of learning and growing. Constructive criticism is meant to show you what you've done well and how you can continue to improve. Here are some tips on how to take criticism constructively, with a touch of humor to lighten the mood.

Tip 1: Listen Carefully

When receiving constructive criticism, it's important to listen carefully to what you're being told. One time, I misinterpreted criticism from a teacher and thought they were attacking me personally. But after I took a moment to listen and understand their perspective, I realized that they were trying to help me improve. So, listen carefully to what the person is saying and try to see it from their point of view.

Tip 2: Don't Get Angry

Dealing with criticism takes maturity and self-control. It can be tempting to get defensive or angry when receiving criticism, but that won't get you anywhere. Instead, take a deep breath and stay calm. Remember that the person is offering you feedback to help you improve.

Tip 3: Show Appreciation

When someone offers you constructive criticism, it's important to show appreciation and thank them for taking the time to look at your work or idea. This can help build a positive relationship and show that you're open to feedback. Don't interrupt to defend yourself; instead, listen to what they have to say and ask questions if needed.

Tip 4: Take Action

Finally, take the criticism seriously and take corrective action as needed. This can be a great opportunity to learn and grow, so don't let it go to waste. Use the feedback to correct mistakes and strive to improve in the future.

Taking criticism constructively takes maturity, self-control, and a willingness to learn and grow. Listen carefully, don't get angry, show appreciation, and take action. By following these tips, you can turn criticism into an opportunity to improve and achieve your goals. Effective communication is a vital skill that can help you achieve success in all aspects of life. By practicing active listening, being clear and concise, showing respect, using body language, and practicing empathy, and taking criticism, you can improve your communication skills and build strong relationships with those around you. And remember, a little bit of humor can make even the most challenging conversations a bit more bearable!

Pitfalls...

Effective communication is crucial for building strong relationships and achieving your goals. However, there are some traps that can hinder effective communication. Here are some common traps to avoid when communicating, with a touch of humor to lighten the mood.

Trap 1: Assuming

Assuming can be a trap that many of us fall into. We assume that the other person knows what we're talking about or that they share our opinions. But assuming can lead to misunderstandings and miscommunication. So, don't assume; instead, communicate clearly and ask questions to ensure mutual understanding.

Trap 2: Interrupting

Have you ever been interrupted mid-sentence? It can be frustrating and can derail the conversation. Interrupting is a trap that can hinder effective communication. So, be patient and wait for the other person to finish speaking before responding.

Trap 3: Blaming

Blaming is another trap that can hinder effective communication. Blaming someone else for a problem or issue can lead to defensiveness and hostility, making it difficult to find a solution. Instead, take responsibility for your actions and focus on finding a solution together.

Trap 4: Over-explaining

Over-explaining can be a trap that can lead to confusion and boredom. When communicating, it's important to be clear and concise. So, avoid over-explaining and focus on the key points. Keep it simple and straightforward.

Trap 5: Ignoring Non-Verbal Cues

Non-verbal cues, such as body language and tone of voice, can provide valuable information about how the other person is feeling. Ignoring these cues can be a trap that can lead to misunderstandings and miscommunication. So, pay attention to the other person's non-verbal cues and respond appropriately.

Effective communication requires avoiding these common traps. Don't assume, interrupt, blame, over-explain, or ignore non-verbal cues. By avoiding these traps, you can communicate more effectively and build stronger relationships.

CHAPTER 6

Bullying is never ok

Have you ever wondered why some people are just plain mean? Why they feel the need to pick on others and make them feel small? I have, and I've come up with a few reasons why people might bully others.

First of all, there's the classic "misery loves company" situation. You know the type – they're unhappy with themselves, so they try to make everyone else unhappy too. It's not right, but it happens.

Then there are the people who just want to be popular, or feel like they need to be in control of a situation. They think that by picking on someone else, they'll look cooler or more powerful. But really, they just look like jerks.

Some people bully others because they've been bullied themselves, and they think that's just how things are supposed to be. It's sad, but it's a vicious cycle.

And finally, there are those who just do it for the fun of it. They find joy in other people's pain, and that's just messed up.

But here's the thing – none of these reasons are good enough to justify bullying someone else. No matter how unhappy or insecure or damaged you may be, you have no right to take that out on someone else. It's not fair, it's not kind, and it's not cool.

I've had my fair share of bullying and wouldn't wish this upon anyone. For me it all started when I was a wee young lass, just a tender 11 years of age. I was the kind of girl who preferred books over boys and homework over hanging out with friends. So, you can imagine my surprise when I found out that I had caught the eye of Karen Midge, the local bully and tormentor extraordinaire.

Karen and her gang of mean girls would make my life a living hell, teasing and taunting me at every turn. They'd pull my hair, steal my lunch, and even went as far as to set my hair on fire with hairspray (let's just say my hair was never the same after that incident).

But as I grew older, I started to realize that Karen's bullying wasn't just some random act of cruelty. There were reasons behind her behavior, reasons that I've come to understand over the years. So, if you've ever wondered why people bully others, here are a few reasons that might shed some light on the subject.

Firstly, some people bully because they themselves have been bullied or abused. They might feel powerless in their own lives and take out their frustrations on others.

Secondly, some people bully because they have low self-esteem and feel the need to put others down in order to make themselves feel better.

Thirdly, some people bully because they crave attention and don't know how to get it in a positive way.

Fourthly, some people bully because they have a need for control and enjoy having power over others.

Finally, some people bully simply because they enjoy it. They find pleasure in making others suffer and it gives them a sense of superiority.

Now, I'm not saying that any of these reasons justify bullying. Bullying is never okay and should never be tolerated. But understanding why someone might bully can help us to better deal with the situation and find ways to overcome it. Fight bullying with your positivity and laughter so here's a joke for you...

Why did the bully refuse to admit to their actions? Because they didn't want to face the punchline! (mic drop...)

~ 8 ~

CHAPTER 7

Building confidence

As a kid, I was about as confident as a cat in a room full of rocking chairs. I was so shy that even speaking up in class was like trying to cross a river of molasses. But, as they say, with great power comes great responsibility, and as I got older, I realized that I needed to take control of my own confidence.

Now, you might be thinking "how does one simply build confidence?" Trust me, it's not as easy as popping a balloon with a needle. It takes time, effort, and a whole lot of self-love.

Firstly, you need to identify your strengths and weaknesses. I, for one, was terrible at sports. My idea of a workout was carrying a stack of books up a flight of stairs. But, I knew that I was great at academics and reading, so I used those strengths to boost my confidence.

Secondly, don't be afraid to try new things! I know it's easier said than done, but trust me, it's worth it. Take a leap of faith and try something that scares you. For me, it was auditioning for the school play. I was petrified of performing in front of people, but I knew I had to step out of my comfort zone. And guess what? I landed the lead role!

Lastly, surround yourself with positive people. Find those who uplift you and encourage you to be your best self. Life's too short to be around people who bring you down. It's like hanging out with a storm cloud on a sunny day. Ain't nobody got time for that!

Remember, building confidence is like building a sandcastle - it takes time, effort, and a lot of trial and error. But with the right tools and mindset, you can build a castle that will stand the test of time. So go out there and build the sandcastle of your dreams, my friends!

And if all else fails, just remember this joke: Why did the tomato turn red? Because it saw the salad dressing! Okay, okay, maybe I'm not the best comedian, but you get the point. Keep smiling, keep laughing, and keep building that confidence! Just for you lovelies, I have listed out the ways you can help build confidence below:

Practice positive self-talk: It's important to change any negative self-talk into positive affirmations. If you catch yourself thinking negatively about yourself, try to turn those thoughts into positive ones.

Focus on your strengths: Everyone has their own unique strengths and abilities. Instead of focusing on your weaknesses, focus on what you're good at and take pride in your abilities.

Set achievable goals: Setting goals can give you a sense of direction and purpose. Make sure to set goals that are realistic and achievable so that you can feel a sense of accomplishment when you achieve them.

Try new things: Trying new things can help you build confidence by stepping out of your comfort zone. When you try something new and succeed, it can help you feel more confident in your abilities.

Celebrate your successes: It's important to celebrate your successes, no matter how small they may be. Recognize your achievements and take pride in them.

Surround yourself with positive people: Surround yourself with people who support you and encourage you to be your best self. Being around positive people can help you feel more confident and motivated.

Take care of yourself: Taking care of your physical and emotional needs can help you feel more confident. Make sure to get enough sleep, eat a healthy diet, and exercise regularly.

Fake it till you make it: Sometimes, you may not feel confident, but acting confident can actually help you feel more confident. Stand up straight, make eye contact, and speak clearly to exude confidence, even if you don't feel it yet.

And always remember, confidence is not something that comes overnight. It takes practice and perseverance. But with these tips, anyone can build their confidence and tackle life's challenges with a positive attitude.

I was once told, "Confidence isn't something that you are born with, it's something that you develop." That stuck with me and helped me realize that even though I lacked confidence as a child, I had the power to build it up. Confidence isn't something that can be given to you by others, it must come from within.

One of the ways to build confidence is to set achievable goals for yourself. As my dad always said, "Rome wasn't built in a day." It's important to take small steps towards your goals and celebrate each accomplishment, no matter how small.

Another way to build confidence is to surround yourself with positive and supportive people. Being around people who believe in you and your abilities can help boost your confidence and motivate you to achieve your goals.

And lastly, it's important to take care of yourself both mentally and physically. Exercise, eat healthy, and get enough rest. When you feel good about yourself, it shows and helps to build your confidence.

As Winston Churchill once said, "Success is not final, failure is not fatal: it is the courage to continue that counts." Building confidence takes time and effort, but with determination and perseverance, anyone can do it.

~ 9 ~

CHAPTER 8

Dealing with bullies

Of course, there's the simple answer that two wrongs don't make a right. For years, Karen tormented me, and I could have easily sunk to her level and fought fire with fire. But I didn't. Instead, I chose to rise above her bullying and take the higher road. I didn't stoop to her level because I knew that would only make me as bad as she was. And even more importantly, I knew that it wouldn't solve anything. It wouldn't make me feel better, and it wouldn't stop Karen from being a bully. In fact, it would probably make things worse. So, I took the difficult but more effective path, and that was to stand up for myself in a respectful and assertive manner, and to seek help from trusted adults when necessary. And while it wasn't always easy, in the end, it was worth it because I was able to come out of the situation with my integrity intact, and Karen's bullying eventually stopped. So, should you use dirty tactics to deal with a bully? No, you shouldn't. Because it's not effective, it's not the right thing to do, and it won't make you feel any better in the long run. Instead, take the higher road and stand up for yourself in a respectful and assertive manner, and don't be afraid to seek help from trusted adults. Trust me, it's worth it in the end.

As I've mentioned earlier, it's never a good idea to use dirty tactics against a bully. However, if you do decide to take action, there are a few things you need to keep in mind.

Firstly, it's important to keep your temper in check. It's easy to get angry and want to lash out, but that will only escalate the situation. Take a deep breath and stay calm. Remember that you're in control of your actions, not the bully.

Secondly, if you decide to gather evidence of the bullying, be sure to do so carefully. Don't stoop to their level and resort to lies or manipulation. Instead, collect evidence in a respectful and honest way. This could be through keeping a diary, recording incidents on your phone, or getting witness statements from others.

Finally, always consider the consequences of your actions. Revenge may feel good in the moment, but it could make things worse for you in the long run. Will the bully retaliate? Will your actions get you in trouble with school authorities? Is there a better way to handle the situation?

By keeping your temper in check, using evidence carefully, and considering your actions, you can navigate the situation in a more mature and effective way. Remember, two wrongs don't make a right.

It wasn't until later in life, when I had learned some valuable lessons, that I was able to effectively deal with bullies. Here are some tips that I have found to be useful:

Firstly, it is important to keep your temper in check. Reacting with anger or aggression will only escalate the situation and could make things worse. Instead, try to remain calm and composed, and respond to the bully in a rational and measured way.

Secondly, use evidence carefully. If you are being bullied, try to gather evidence of the bullying behavior. This could be in the form of witness statements, text messages or emails, or even video footage. Presenting this evidence to an authority figure, such as a teacher or supervisor, can be very effective in getting the bully to stop.

Lastly, always consider what you do. Revenge may seem tempting, but it is rarely the best course of action. It can lead to further escalation of the situation and may even result in legal consequences. Instead, focus on protecting yourself and getting help from others who can support you.

Dealing with bullies can be a challenging experience, but by keeping your temper in check, using evidence carefully, and always considering your actions, you can take control of the situation and stop the bullying for good.

I remember one time when Karen had gone too far and physically hurt me. I knew I had to stand up to her, but I also knew that using violence was not the answer. Instead, I confronted her calmly and explained how her actions were hurting me. Surprisingly, she listened, and we were able to come to a truce. It's important to remember that physical violence is never the answer, and there are always other ways to deal with bullies.

Keeping a record of what a bully does is important for several reasons. Firstly, it can be used as evidence if you need to report the bullying to a teacher or other authority figure. Secondly, it helps to keep track of patterns and identify triggers for the bullying. Lastly, it can be cathartic to get all your thoughts and feelings down on paper.

Sometimes, bullies may be going through their own issues that are causing them to act out. In these cases, referring them to help can be beneficial for both parties. It's important to remember that bullies are people too and may need help dealing with their emotions.

Dealing with bullying can be draining, so it's important to take care of yourself as well. Talk to someone you trust, whether that's a friend, family member, or professional. Find healthy outlets for your emotions, such as exercise or creative hobbies. Most importantly, don't blame yourself for the actions of the bully.

It can be easy to get bogged down in negative thoughts and feelings when dealing with a bully. However, focusing on the positive things in your life can help you build resilience and keep a healthy mindset. Take time to practice gratitude, focus on your strengths and accomplishments, and surround yourself with positive influences.

Taking care of your physical health can have a big impact on your mental wellbeing. Make sure to eat a balanced diet, exercise regularly, and get enough sleep. Additionally, practicing mindfulness and relaxation techniques can help you manage stress and anxiety.

Remember, dealing with bullies can be difficult, but it's important to take care of yourself and seek help if necessary. With the right strategies, you can overcome bullying and come out stronger on the other side.

~ 10 ~

CHAPTER 9

Revenge is sweet

Bullying can be a tough thing to deal with, but fear not my friends! I'm here to give you my top 10 tips on how to deal with those bullies once and for all. So, sit back, grab a cup of tea and let's get started on how to kick those bullies out of your life! I was fed up with Karen Midge and her cronies making my life a living hell. So, I decided to put my brains to use and come up with a plan.

I went straight to the headmaster's office and spilled the beans about Karen and her gang's bullying tactics. It turned out that I wasn't the only victim of their torment. The headmaster called Karen and her parents in for a meeting, and let's just say that Karen's parents were not happy campers.

Karen was forced to apologize to me and the other victims, and her parents made her promise to never bully again. And as for me? Well, I walked out of that meeting with my head held high and a newfound confidence.

It wasn't an easy victory, but it was worth it. I proved to myself that I had the strength and the smarts to stand up to my bullies and make a difference. And that, my friends, is how I got my sweet, sweet revenge.

Now, just for you, my lovelies, I'm going to give you my top ten tips on how to deal with bullies:

Turn the tables: Become a master of puns and comebacks. When the bully says something hurtful, reply with a witty one-liner. For example, when Karen told me I was ugly, I told her she must be jealous of my stunning personality.

Stand up straight: good posture exudes confidence. Even if you're feeling like a scared little mouse on the inside, standing up straight can make you look and feel more powerful.

Find an ally: Bullies are often cowards who feel emboldened by a lack of resistance. Find someone who can be your wingman (or wingwoman) and provide support when you need it.

Be assertive: Don't be afraid to tell the bully that their behavior is unacceptable. Speak in a clear, calm voice and stand your ground.

Document everything: Keep a record of the bullying incidents, including the date, time, and what was said or done. This can be useful evidence if you need to report the bully to an authority figure.

Don't engage: Sometimes the best way to deal with a bully is to simply ignore them. Don't give them the satisfaction of knowing they've gotten under your skin.

Speak up: If you're being physically hurt or feel like your safety is in danger, don't hesitate to tell someone in authority, whether it's a teacher, parent, or other adult.

Take care of yourself: Bullying can take a toll on your mental health. Make sure to practice self-care, whether it's through exercise, talking to a trusted friend, or seeking help from a therapist.

Stay positive: Remember that you're not alone and that bullying doesn't define you. Focus on your strengths and the things you enjoy.

Keep a sense of humor: Laughter can be a powerful antidote to bullying. Find ways to inject humor into your life, whether it's through watching funny videos or reading humorous books. And remember, as Terry Pratchett once said, "If you can't laugh at yourself, you're missing the best joke of all."

So, there you have it, my top ten proven tips to help you deal with bullies. Reminds me of my grandfather and his wise words...

"And always remember," my grandpa used to say, "never fight fire with fire unless you're a dragon. Otherwise, you'll just end up with a lot of burnt feathers and a very angry goose." So, stay calm, stay cool, and use these ten tips to deal with bullies without getting burnt!

~ 11 ~

CHAPTER 10

Everyday life skills

Helping around the house...

As part of a family, you are an important part of household activities, so doing your part in daily and weekly chores is normal. Each family member is responsible for doing their fair share.

Chores help keep your home clean and comfortable. They also teach you about responsibility, which is something that will always be part of life. You'll also learn about what it takes to keep a household running smoothly, and you'll become familiar with the great feeling of a job well done.

Not every chore is pleasant to take care of, but it makes life more pleasant when it's finished. This is a bit like bathing yourself regularly-it may not be your favorite thing to do, but it sure beats the alternative! So, resolve to make peace with your chores. One way or another, they need to be done, or one morning you may find yourself eating breakfast from a greasy, crusty plate because last night's dinner dishes weren't washed.

Silver linings...

I like to think of myself as a self-proclaimed expert on the topic of chores. Some people might roll their eyes at the thought of vacuuming or doing laundry, but not me. I've come to realize that there are actually some pretty great benefits to doing chores that I'd like to share with you.

Sense of accomplishment: There's nothing like the feeling of crossing a chore off your to-do list. It's almost as satisfying as getting a gold star in kindergarten. Now if only someone would give me a sticker every time I fold a load of laundry...

Stress-reliever: Who needs therapy when you have a sink full of dirty dishes to wash? I mean, sure, it's not quite the same as lying on a couch and spilling your deepest, darkest fears to a stranger, but it's cheaper and your kitchen will be sparkling clean afterwards.

Exercise: Who needs a personal trainer when you have a house that needs cleaning? I mean, have you ever tried to scrub a stubborn stain off a countertop? It's basically like doing a bicep curl, but with a sponge. Plus, you get to wear your comfiest clothes, and nobody judges you for your sweat stains.

Saves money: Forget about those fancy cleaning products and gadgets. All you need is some good old-fashioned elbow grease and maybe a bit of vinegar. And the best part? You get to keep all the money you save to spend on something really important, like a new pair of shoes.

Can be enjoyable/fun: Sure, doing chores might not be the most glamorous activity in the world, but that doesn't mean you can't make it fun. Turn on some music, bust out your best dance moves, and before you know it, you'll be having a party in your living room. Who needs a nightclub when you can twirl a mop around like a pro?"

Hopefully, doing chores will now seem a little less tedious and a lot more enjoyable.

Spread your wings...

As a former teenager myself, I know that feeling of wanting to spread your wings and gain more independence. Luckily, there are ways to do just that, and the benefits are pretty sweet. So, whether you're dying to stay out past curfew or just want to be trusted with the car keys, here are my top tips for gaining more independence:

Communicate: Talk to your parents or guardians about your desire for more independence. Explain why you feel ready for it and what you hope to gain from it. They may be more willing to give you some freedom if they understand where you're coming from.

Take responsibility: Show your parents that you can be responsible by completing your chores and homework on time, keeping your room tidy, and following the rules. When they see that you're reliable, they may be more likely to trust you with bigger responsibilities.

Show maturity: Act maturely and respectfully towards your parents and others. Show that you can handle yourself in different situations, and they may be more willing to let you handle things on your own.

Be patient: Gaining more independence takes time, and you may need to prove yourself over a period of time before your parents are comfortable giving you more freedom. So, be patient and keep working at it.

Enjoy the benefits: Once you've gained more independence, enjoy it! You'll have more control over your own life, be able to make your own decisions, and learn valuable life skills. Plus, you'll have the satisfaction of knowing that you've earned your parents' trust and respect.

With a little communication, responsibility, maturity, patience, and a positive attitude, you'll be well on your way to gaining more independence and all the benefits that come with it. Just remember, with great independence comes great responsibility... and a whole lot of laundry. But hey, at least you get to pick out your own detergent, right?

Fail to plan; plan to fail...

I know how tough it can be for kids to manage their time effectively. But fear not, my friends, for I have some tips and tricks up my sleeve to help you stay on top of things. So, grab a snack and settle in for some time-management wisdom...

Use a planner: Get yourself a planner and write down everything you need to do. Trust me, it's like a magic spell for your brain. Seeing everything laid out in front of you can help you prioritize and manage your time more effectively. Plus, it's a great excuse to buy some cute stationery.

Break tasks into smaller chunks: Have a big project or assignment due? Don't try to tackle it all at once. Break it down into smaller, more manageable chunks, and work on them one at a time. It'll feel less overwhelming, and you'll actually be able to make progress without wanting to pull your hair out.

Eliminate distractions: Ah, social media, the ultimate time-suck. If you find yourself getting distracted by Instagram or TikTok, put your phone in another room or use an app that blocks certain websites during study time. And if you really can't resist the urge to scroll, at least make it educational and follow some cool science or history accounts.

Prioritize self-care: Yes, managing your time effectively means making time for self-care too. Schedule in some relaxation time, whether it's taking a bubble bath, going for a walk, or binge-watching your favorite show. You'll come back to your work feeling refreshed and ready to tackle it.

Don't procrastinate: And last but not least, the most important tip of all: don't procrastinate. I know, I know, easier said than done. But trust me, putting things off until the last minute is a surefire way to stress yourself out and end up with subpar work. And as someone who once wrote a paper on Shakespeare the night before it was due and ended up accidentally referring to him as "Shark-spear", take it from me, it's not worth it.

Follow these tips and you'll be a time-management master in no time. And if all else fails, just remember: Rome wasn't built in a day, but it was built with a lot of planning and organization.

~ 12 ~

CHAPTER 11

Money, money, money

Now, let's get on to everyone's favorite topic: money. As a former broke college student who once survived solely on ramen noodles and instant coffee, I know firsthand how important it is to learn how to manage your money. There's nothing quite like the feeling of staring at your bank account balance and realizing you only have enough money left to buy a single ply roll of toilet paper. But don't worry, I'm here to help. So, without further ado, here are my top tips on how to become a money-management wizard.

Money management...

Make a budget: Sit down and make a budget listing all your expenses and income. It may seem like a boring task, but knowing where your money is going is the first step to managing it like a boss. And who knows, maybe you'll find out you have more money to spend on the things you love than you thought!

Save, save, save: You don't have to be a millionaire to save money. Start putting some of your cash away in a savings account for a rainy day. Even if it's just a few dollars a week, it'll add up over time. And let's be real, who wouldn't want a stash of cash to spend on their next vacation or new outfit?

Avoid debt: Credit cards may seem cool, but if you're not careful, they can lead to some serious debt. Stick to using cash or a debit card, and only use a credit card if you can pay it off in full each month. Trust me, you don't want to end up like those people on TV who owe thousands of dollars to their credit card companies.

Be a smart shopper: Nobody wants to pay full price for anything, am I right? Always look for deals and discounts before making a purchase, and don't be afraid to negotiate. And if you're feeling really thrifty, try using coupons. It's like a game, but instead of winning points, you get to save money!

Invest in yourself: You don't have to be a genius to be successful, but it helps to invest in yourself. Take classes or learn new skills that can help you earn more money in the future. Plus, learning new things is pretty cool, too.

Seek advice: It's okay to ask for help! Talk to someone you trust, like a parent, teacher, or financial advisor, if you need advice on how to manage your money. They may have some cool tips or tricks you haven't thought of.

Learn from your mistakes: And last but not least, don't beat yourself up if you make a financial mistake. We all make them! The important thing is to learn from them and make a plan to avoid making the same mistake twice. And remember, it's never too late to start being smart with your money.

I know most of you are not quite ready for all of the above and most parents will manage the household money, but with these easy steps, you can be on your way to becoming a money-management ninja in no time. Who knows, maybe you'll be the one giving financial advice to your friends someday!"

High roller...

I know how frustrating it can be to not have your own money. Luckily, there are plenty of ways for teens to earn some cash and feel like a true baller. So, without further ado, here are my top 7 ways for teens to make some dough:

Babysitting: If you're good with kids and know how to change a diaper, then babysitting could be your calling. Parents are always in need of a night out, and they'll be happy to pay someone responsible to watch their little ones. Plus, if you're lucky, the kids might even go to bed early and you can catch up on your Netflix shows.

Dog walking: Who doesn't love dogs? If you're a fan of our furry friends, then dog walking could be a great way to make some money while getting some exercise. Just make sure you're not allergic to pet hair!

Lawn mowing: If you don't mind getting your hands dirty, then lawn mowing could be a great way to earn some cash. Ask your neighbors if they need their lawn mowed, or post an ad on social media. You'll be making money and getting a killer tan at the same time.

House cleaning: Cleaning isn't everyone's favorite activity, but if you're good at it, you can make some serious cash. Offer to clean your neighbors' homes, or post an ad on Craigslist. And who knows, maybe you'll discover a love for organizing that you never knew you had.

Tutoring: Are you a math whiz or a history buff? If so, then tutoring could be your ticket to making some extra cash. Offer to tutor classmates or younger kids in your neighborhood or post an ad online. Plus, you'll be helping others succeed in school, which is pretty cool.

Selling stuff online: If you have a lot of stuff lying around your room that you don't use anymore, consider selling it online. Websites like eBay and Depop are great places to sell your clothes, accessories, and other items you no longer need. Just make sure to get your parents' permission before selling anything.

Odd jobs: If none of the above options sound like your cup of tea, then consider offering your services for odd jobs. This could include anything from helping someone move furniture to painting a fence. Just be sure to negotiate a fair price and don't take on anything you're not comfortable with.

You can be well on your way to earning some serious cash. And who knows, maybe someday you'll be the next Mark Zuckerberg, who started Facebook in his college dorm room and became one of the richest people in the world. Just remember, every successful entrepreneur started somewhere, so don't be afraid to get creative and think outside the box.

~ 13 ~

CHAPTER 12

Your Passport to the future

I was always a curious kid who loved to learn new things. I was always asking questions, reading books, and exploring the world around me. But when it came to studying, I wasn't always the most enthusiastic. I mean, let's be real, who wants to spend hours reading a textbook when there are so many cute cat videos on YouTube?

One day, my teacher assigned a big project that would require a lot of research and studying. I groaned at the thought of all the time I'd have to spend pouring over books and websites. But then, my teacher reminded me of the importance of studying.

"If you want to learn and grow, you have to put in the work," my teacher said. "Studying helps you understand the material, improves your problem-solving skills, and boosts your confidence."

I thought about what my teacher said and realized that I did want to learn and grow. So, I got to work on my project, researching and studying for hours on end. And you know what? It wasn't as bad as I thought it would be. Sure, my eyes may have crossed a few times from staring at my computer screen, but I also learned some pretty cool stuff.

As I worked on the project, I discovered all sorts of new things that I never would have known otherwise. Did you know that a group of flamingos is called a flamboyance? Or that the shortest war in history lasted only 38 minutes? Yeah, I didn't either.

And the more I studied, the more I realized how important it was to keep learning and growing. Plus, let's be real, knowing random facts like the ones I just mentioned can come in handy at parties.

Years later, I looked back on that project as a turning point in my life. It was the moment when I realized the true importance of studying, even if it meant missing out on some cute cat videos. I went on to study hard in school, land a great job, and become a successful entrepreneur. And I owe it all to that one project and my teacher's wise words.

So, if you're ever feeling like skipping studying, just remember that it's not all bad. Sure, there may be some boring parts, but you never know what cool and random facts you might learn. And who knows, maybe someday those facts will come in handy and make you the star of a party! Here are just some of the reasons why education is probably the most crucial thing you do in your life:

Better grades: Okay, this one's a no-brainer. Studying helps you learn and understand the material, which translates into better grades. And let's be real, who doesn't want to impress their parents with an A on their report card?

Improved job prospects: Whether you want to be a doctor or a rock star, studying is essential to achieving your career goals. Most jobs require some level of education, so the more you study, the more likely you are to land your dream job.

Increased knowledge: Studying isn't just about getting good grades or getting a job. It's also about gaining knowledge and expanding your horizons. You never know what you might learn that could come in handy someday.

Better problem-solving skills: Studying helps you develop critical thinking and problem-solving skills. These skills will serve you well in all aspects of life, from tackling a tough homework assignment to figuring out how to fix a broken car.

Boosted confidence: When you study and understand the material, you'll feel more confident in yourself and your abilities. And confidence is key to success in all areas of life.

Studying may not be the most exciting thing in the world, but it's super important for your future success.

Effective learning...

As someone who loves to learn new things, I know that finding the right learning method can make all the difference. So, without further ado, here are my top 5 learning methods:

Reading and Writing: If you're someone who learns best by reading and writing, then this method is for you. Reading books, articles, and other materials can help you absorb new information, while writing notes or creating outlines can help you organize your thoughts and remember what you've learned. Plus, if you're a fan of puns like me, you can always sneak a few into your notes to make studying a bit more fun.

Visual aids: Some people learn best by seeing, so visual aids can be super helpful. This could include things like diagrams, charts, and videos. And if you're a fan of memes, you'll be happy to know that they can be a great way to visualize and remember information.

Repetition: Repetition may seem boring, but it's actually a great way to learn and remember information. Whether it's repeating a phrase out loud or writing it down multiple times, repetition can help you retain information and make it stick.

Group learning: If you're someone who likes to bounce ideas off of others, then group learning is for you. This could include things like study groups, discussion panels, or even just chatting with friends about a topic. Just make sure to keep the group focused - it's easy to get sidetracked talking about the latest TikTok trend.

Learning through games: Who says learning has to be boring? Learning through games can be a fun and effective way to absorb new information. Whether it's a trivia game or a simulation, games can help you learn without even realizing it. And who knows, you might even be able to convince your parents that playing video games is actually productive."

Use whichever method works for you but remember, education is super important, but that doesn't mean it has to be boring. As Albert Einstein once said, 'Education is what remains after one has forgotten what one has learned in school.' So go ahead, have fun with your learning, and who knows, you might just discover something new and amazing."...

Creative spaces...

I remember back in high school, I used to try to study in my messy bedroom with the TV on and my phone buzzing every two seconds. Needless to say, I didn't retain much information. But once I started creating a better learning environment, I saw a huge improvement in my grades and my overall understanding of the material. So, without further ado, here are 5 key components of the ideal environment for effective learning."

Comfortable furniture: Let's face it, nobody likes sitting on an uncomfortable chair for hours on end. Make sure your learning environment has comfortable furniture, whether it's a cozy armchair, a supportive desk chair, or even a bean bag chair. Just try not to fall asleep if you go for the bean bag option.

Good lighting: The right lighting can make all the difference when it comes to studying. Make sure your environment has plenty of natural light or bright, adjustable lamps. And if you're feeling adventurous, you can even invest in some color-changing light bulbs for a fun study vibe.

Minimal distractions: Distractions can be a real productivity killer, so try to minimize them as much as possible. This could mean turning off your phone, closing unnecessary tabs on your computer, or even wearing noise-cancelling headphones. Just be careful not to crank up the music too loud and start singing along.

Good air quality: Breathing in fresh air can help you stay alert and focused, so make sure your learning environment has good air quality. Open a window if you can or invest in an air purifier. And if you're feeling extra fancy, you can even add some plants for a natural air purifier and a pop of color.

Organized space: A cluttered space can lead to a cluttered mind, so make sure your learning environment is well-organized. Keep your books, notes, and other materials tidy and easy to access. And if you're feeling really ambitious, you can even color-code your notes for maximum organization.

These are my top 5 components of the ideal environment for effective learning. Whether you're studying for a test, learning a new skill, or just trying to expand your knowledge, creating the right environment can make all the difference. Now go ahead, create your ideal learning space, and get ready to learn like a boss.

Don't worry, be happy...

I remember feeling overwhelmed with schoolwork, friendships, and just life in general. It seemed like every day was a new challenge, and it was easy to get bogged down by negativity. But over time, I learned some tips and tricks that helped me stay positive, even when things got tough. I want to share some of the tips that helped me to stay positive during my worst years of bullying in school:

Focus on the good: It can be easy to get caught up in negative thoughts and feelings but try to shift your focus to the good things in your life. Maybe you have a supportive family, great friends, or a hobby you love. Take some time to appreciate and be grateful for these things.

Surround yourself with positivity: The people you spend time with can have a big impact on your mindset. Try to surround yourself with positive, supportive people who lift you up and make you feel good about yourself. And if you come across negative people or situations, try to distance yourself or find ways to cope.

Take care of yourself: Taking care of your physical and mental health is key to staying positive. Make sure you're getting enough sleep, eating healthy foods, and staying active. And don't be afraid to ask for help if you're struggling with mental health issues like anxiety or depression.

Practice self-compassion: It's easy to be hard on yourself, especially as a teenager. But practicing self-compassion can help you stay positive and motivated. Try to be kind and forgiving to yourself, and remember that mistakes and setbacks are a natural part of life.

Find a creative outlet: Engaging in a creative activity like writing, drawing, or music can be a great way to stay positive and express yourself. Plus, it can be a fun and rewarding way to relieve stress and boost your mood.

Remember, staying positive is a journey, not a destination. It takes practice and effort, but it's worth it in the end. With the right mindset and some helpful tips, you can stay positive even in the face of the most difficult challenges and adversity. And who knows, maybe someday you'll be the one giving advice on how to stay positive. Just don't forget to throw in a few cheesy jokes to make it fun.

~ 14 ~

CHAPTER 13

End of the road

Learning life skills is essential for teenagers as it helps them navigate the ups and downs of adulthood with confidence. Money management skills, including budgeting, saving, and investing, are crucial for becoming financially responsible. Seeking out resources and support can make the daunting process more manageable. Additionally, dealing with bullies is an unfortunate reality for many teenagers. Speaking up and seeking help from a trusted adult can help stop the bullying and keep the individual safe. Cultivating a love of learning is also important for personal growth and development. Trying new things and stepping out of one's comfort zone can lead to a rewarding experience.

Overall, learning life skills like money management, dealing with bullies, and learning itself can be empowering and enriching experiences. They can help teenagers take control of their lives, stand up for themselves, and continue to grow and develop throughout their lives. With the right mindset and a willingness to learn, the sky's the limit!

And that's a wrap, guys! I hope this book has been helpful in teaching you some important life skills that will serve you well in the future. Remember, learning these skills is not only practical, but also empowering. You have the ability to take charge of your life, make informed decisions, and navigate the ups and downs of adulthood with confidence. Whether you're learning to manage your money, organize your time, or stay positive, these skills will be invaluable as you grow and develop. And who knows, maybe someday you'll be the one writing a book on how to be a successful adult. Just don't forget to give me a shoutout in the acknowledgments. Thanks for reading and go out there and crush it!

~ 15 ~

ABOUT THE AUTHOR

Isabella Thorne is an author who has a passion for writing about personal growth, self-improvement, and living a fulfilling life. She believes that everyone has the potential to be their best self, and her writing is focused on helping readers unlock that potential.

Isabella's journey as a writer began in her teenage years when she started keeping a journal to document her experiences and emotions. This eventually led her to explore the world of self-help and personal development, and she began writing about these topics to share her insights and experiences with others.

Isabella is committed to writing in a style that is engaging, relatable, and accessible to all readers. Her goal is to inspire and motivate others to take control of their lives and achieve their goals, no matter how big or small.

In addition to writing, Isabella enjoys traveling, hiking, and spending time with her family and friends. She is also an avid reader and loves to learn about new topics and ideas.

Whether you're looking to improve your finances, overcome bullying, or simply learn new skills, Isabella's writing is a valuable resource for anyone looking to lead a more fulfilling life.

www.ingramcontent.com/pod-product-compliance
Lightning Source LLC
Chambersburg PA
CBHW070119110526
44587CB00015BA/2665